"This we know: the Earth does not belong to man;
man belongs to the Earth. Man did not weave the web of life,
he is merely a strand woven in it.
Whatever he does to the web, he does to himself.
All things are connected like the blood that unites one family.
All things are connected."

ALL THINGS CONNECTED

Native American Creations

SELECTIONS FROM THE NATIVE AMERICAN COLLECTION

THE MUSEUM OF NATURAL HISTORY, ROGER WILLIAMS PARK

PROVIDENCE, RHODE ISLAND

COVER

Jar-shaped Basket (Olla), Southwest, Western Apache, 1890-1910

Willow, cottonwood and martynia, 20 in. high x 49 in. circumference

Exchange; Museum of the American Indian, E 1154 1945

"Little dogs" and "crosses" or "stars" are scattered around stacked,

irregular diamonds, giving this jar-shaped basket a lively look.

Here asymmetrical placement of elements—which is typical of many

Western Apache examples—serves to heighten aesthetic interest.

FRONTISPIECE

Members of the Narragansett tribe gather on the steps of the

museum, circa 1920. From the museum archives.

FRONTISPIECE QUOTATION

Chief Seattle; spoken to a tribal assembly prior to signing

the Indian Treaties in 1854.

Published by The Museum of Natural History,
Roger Williams Park, Providence, Rhode Island.

This catalogue was published in conjunction with the exhibition
All Things Connected: Native American Creations, on
view at the Museum of Natural History, Roger Williams Park,
10 June 1995 through 5 April 1997.

ISBN 0-9646544-0-7

Printed in the USA

TABLE OF CONTENTS

ACKNOWLEDGEMENTS

FOR THE MUSEUM OF NATURAL HISTORY, ROGER WILLIAMS PARK, our first exhibit catalogue comes in the last year of the museum's first century. Some of the objects from the collection which are included in the exhibit and in this catalogue were last seen by the public during the 1970s.

Of the many people who contributed to the success of this project, a special thank you goes to Mayor Vincent A. Cianci, Jr. for his continuing support of the museum. I would also like to thank my immediate predecessor, Elizabeth R.T. Fradin, who spearheaded the museum's recent revival with great determination. The inspiration for the catalogue came from Superintendent of Parks Nancy L. Derrig, whose steady hand guided the project through a host of obstacles. The effort that has gone into the production of this catalogue reflects its title. All things *are* connected. The work linked its creators to creators of the past, and its content links the dominant culture to its original host, the Native American culture itself.

Much of the analysis and interpretation that permitted the museum to bring its Native American collection up to modern technical and intellectual standards after decades in storage was the work of Curator Marilyn Massaro and Associate Curator of Ethnology Kristine Hastreiter. Generous advice and support came from two Native Americans. Dr. Doris Norman (Morningstar) of the North American Indian Center of Boston provided valuable insight and direction. And the Rhode Island Indian Council's Paulla Dove Jennings provided the necessary link with the local Native American community. Part of that community is Joanne Wilcox, our administrative assistant, whose technical expertise and good cheer made it possible to process the stacks of paperwork such a project inevitably inspires. All things are connected to Joanne.

Considerable assistance in identifying and interpreting the objects was provided by Sarah Peabody Turnbaugh of the Museum of Primitive Art and Culture, in Peace Dale, R.I., and Barbara Hail and Thierry Gentis of the Haffenreffer Museum of Anthropology, in Bristol, R.I. Valuable artistic and design input came from Ira Garber and Nicole Juen. Editing and copyreading services were donated by David Brussat. This exhibit and catalogue would still be no more than expert analysis without the dedicated labor of Carolyn Riccardelli, A. Alexandra O'Donnell, David Santilli, Normand Wolf, Linda Eppich, Michael Kieron, Heather Burrows, Kristen Reynolds, Raquel Benros, Todd Provost, Michael Corrente and Josephine Martens.

Finally, the exhibit was funded wholly through the generosity of the Champlin Foundation, another example of its dedication to the citizens of the State of Rhode Island. For, indeed, all things are connected.

TRACEY K. BRUSSAT, MUSEUM DIRECTOR

Roger Williams Park Museum, circa 1910.

Photographed by Theodore Datz.

From the collection of Gladys Bailey.

THE SELECTION OF NATIVE NORTH AMERICAN MATERIAL culture catalogued in these pages is part of the collections first presented almost a century ago by the founders of the Museum of Natural History, Roger Williams Park, which opened in 1896. The objects were last on view in an exhibit that opened in 1958. Not long after that exhibit closed, the museum itself languished, as the population of the city of Providence shifted increasingly to the suburbs. Benefiting from the city's recent artistic and cultural renaissance, this exhibit and catalogue represent the culmination of a ten-year renewal program at the museum in preparation for its centennial in 1996.

Between the first and the current exhibition of these objects, much has changed in the culture of museums and the way collections are presented. That metamorphosis is the subject of the introduction by Gary Zabel that follows. This preface offers the reader a brief history of the Museum of Natural History and its collections as background for the introduction and the catalogue itself.

In June of 1896, when the museum opened, the public beheld a building intended not merely to house a collection of mounted mammals and birds. It was a monument to science and the embodiment of a national, indeed an international movement dedicated to natural history collecting, both amateur and professional. The movement led to the construction of museums in major cities around the nation. These typically were grand structures reflecting Victorian exuberance. Many were built in urban parks created as part of the City Beautiful Movement then reaching its peak in America.

The museum in Providence was situated on the highest prospect of Roger Williams Park, designed in 1878 by Horace W.S. Cleveland, a colleague of Frederick Law Olmsted, the architect of Central Park in New York City. Olmsted was a chief proponent of the urban park movement that grew out of the City Beautiful Movement. Alas, neither movement much outlasted the First World War, but each left a legacy testifying to the era's high hopes and aspirations. In Providence, Roger Williams Park and its museum are two such treasures. Both are listed on the National Register of Historic Places.

The museum was conceived in 1892, in response to a donation of 250 mammal and bird specimens collected by a former resident of Providence, John Steere, of Santa Monica, California. Steere's bequest stipulated that the collection be housed in "a suitable building." In the decades following the museum's opening in 1896, his collection was augmented by donations from amateur collectors and their families. Many collections were amassed in Rhode Island and around the nation as industrial prosperity created a genuine middle class of unparalleled wealth and leisure. In the age before the automobile and the radio, collecting was a common diversion of the middle and upper-middle class. The park and its museum offered citizens of Providence a novel place to visit, and by the thousands they came in fair weather via carriage, trolley, and eventually by automobile.

In its first two decades, so many collections were donated to the museum, and so popular were its exhibitions, that in 1915 a new wing was built. The exhibits expanded to include privately amassed collections of mounted flora and fauna, minerals, fossils and "relics" of archaeology, donated by Charles Gorton, a bookkeeper who lived his entire life on Friendship Street, and James Angus, of West Farms, New York, whose donation was made in memory of his brother-in-law, city auditor William Nisbet, of Pitman Street.

In 1921, a major augmentation of the museum's collections resulted from the demise of the Providence Franklin Society, a century-old club of privileged gentlemen, many of whom were amateur naturalists and collectors. Headquartered at the Providence Athenaeum after its construction in 1838 on Benefit Street, the society had contributed to the intellectual vitality of the city, providing a site for erudite lectures and a home for its collection of natural "curiosities." Over the years, changing social customs diminished its membership, and when the society voted to shut down, most of its collection was donated to the museum. The bulk consisted of some 400 ethnographic objects from the island cultures of the South Pacific—the first cultural artifacts in the museum's hitherto almost exclusively natural collections.

Construction of the museum's north wing nears completion in July 1915. From the museum archives.

This kept the museum abreast of developments in the field, in which the role of natural collections as educational tools was enhanced by the presentation of artifacts from cultures existing close to nature. Indeed, the evolution of anthropology as a discipline in the United States was closely linked to the growth of natural history museums. The course of anthropological study was shaped in particular by the Smithsonian Institution, which was linked to the Bureau of American Ethnology, and by the American Museum of Natural History in New York City, the Field Museum in Chicago, and a growing number of museums connected to universities.

Anthropology developed as a branch of the natural sciences. Because no course of formal training yet existed in the field of anthropology, its American pioneers adopted the highly descriptive and comparative methods of natural history: documenting, classifying and systematizing the cultures of non-European society as they did the natural world. The tradition of gathering cultural objects along with plant, animal and mineral specimens was already well established by the time the Franklin Society relinquished its holdings to the museum in 1921.

The cultural collections contain approximately 24,000 items, the bulk consisting of some 20,000 Native North American stone implements. The remaining 4,000 ethnographic objects include pottery, pipes, baskets, weaponry, clothing, furniture and other items donated by the original owners or their descendants.

The ethnographic items are primarily of Pacific Island and North American origin, the latter donated near the turn of the century by such prominent local residents as Gen. Charles Abbott, A. H. Anderson, Ellen M. Anthony, Daniel B. Fearing, Everet W. Freeman, Dr. Roland Hammond, J.C. Kransoff D.M.D., Mrs. Mary C. P. Parker, Henry D. Sharpe, Justice Charles F. Stearns, H.A. Sweetland, Mrs. Lydia Talbot and James Vaughn. Thereafter, the largest single ethnographic donation, over 50 objects, was loaned to the museum by Walter G. Brown, a Providence investment broker, in 1917 (accessioned formally in 1960). Additional Native American objects were secured through exchange with and/or purchase from the Smithsonian, the Heye Foundation's Museum of the American Indian, Dartmouth College Museum in Hanover, New Hampshire, and Brown University's dispersed Jenks Museum and its Haffenreffer Museum of Anthropology, in Bristol, Rhode Island.

The museum's Native American collection features material from tribes in the Northeast, Plains, Southwest, Northwest Coast, Subarctic and Arctic. Although some earlier objects are included, the collection dates primarily from 1850 to 1950. As this period encompasses the later westward expansion of the United States, it includes artifacts collected from tribes before and after their extensive contact with European-oriented cultures, including wares fabricated for the 20th-century tourist trade. Because the collection grew from diverse sources, its scope is not dictated by any one anthropological goal, or by the interests of any collector or donor. This permits the museum staff to interpret the collection as an artifact in and of itself—a collective effort, as it were, by Rhode Islanders, who in the course of a century have shaped a cultural treasure.

Although consisting of much the same material, the current Native American exhibit catalogued herein may be considered a distant relative of its immediate ancestor. That exhibit, entitled "Hall of the American Indian and Eskimo," was installed on the second floor of the museum in 1958, under the guidance of Horace Wilcox of the University Museum of Archaeology and Anthropology, at the University of Pennsylvania in Philadelphia. Its mahogany-and-glass exhibit cases were filled with "Indian trophies and relics." Dioramas and mannequins augmented the presentation of objects, and the exhibit text divided the objects into strict regional cultures—a style no longer considered sufficiently reflective of the intermingling and migratory habits of most Native American peoples.

Traditionally, museums have tended to think of exhibits (and catalogues) as conforming to one of two models: either as vehicles for the presentation of objects, or as space for the telling of a story. With this exhibit, the museum embraces a new model. Gone are the dioramas, the unintelligible monographs and uninterpretive labels segregating cultural groups into niches or micro-habitats. This exhibit occupies a more neutral interpretive environment. Here, the visitor is invited to read text that places the objects in aesthetic and cultural context, but he or she is allowed the opportunity to confront stereotypes, compare perspectives and draw his or her own aesthetic and cultural conclusions.

Our objective is to showcase the museum's collection of Native American material culture, and to expose the public to issues surrounding the relationship of museums to the cultures they presume to interpret. With this exhibit, the museum has joined that debate. The mere act of placing an object on exhibit changes the object's status. Subtle messages conveyed through the method of presentation can enhance or impede the appreciation of an object's aesthetic, cultural, social, historical and political significance.

And, for that matter, some objects are too sacred to be exhibited to the public. This last issue has been addressed by the federal Native American Graves Protection and Repatriation Act of 1990, which gives Native American tribes the right to reclaim objects long housed in museums around the nation. Some objects have been excluded from this exhibit and catalogue for reasons of cultural patrimony or spiritual signifigance.

With the advent of the National Museum of the American Indian as part of the Smithsonian Institution, these and other relevant concerns have come to a head. The Museum of Natural History looks forward to shedding old roles and paving new ground in the interpretation and exhibition of Native American and other material cultures.

As the museum prepares for its second century, the curatorial staff has begun to take stock of its collections and to reflect upon the various roles it has played as an institution over the span of decades. The museum collects natural history specimens and cultural artifacts, assembled primarily by local collectors from sites around the world. We care for and conserve what has been entrusted to us, and use it to teach and inspire the public. From its inception as a repository of Rhode Island flora and fauna, the museum assumed the role of "People's University" during the first half of the 20th century and, in part, that of a folk art and Hmong cultural center in the late 1970s and early 1980s. As we approach our centennial the Museum of Natural History, Roger Williams Park, reaffirms its mission as the "People's University": an informal education center open to all, and to which all are welcome.

MARILYN MASSARO, CURATOR OF COLLECTIONS, AND
KRISTINE L. HASTREITER, ASSOCIATE CURATOR OF ETHNOLOGY
MUSEUM OF NATURAL HISTORY

INTRODUCTION

Installation of the "Hall of the American
Indian and Eskimo," 1957.
Courtesy of The Providence Journal.

IN THIS CATALOGUE AND THE EXHIBITION IT ACCOMPANIES, the staff of the Museum of Natural History, Roger Williams Park presents the Native American objects in its collection as works of art. This is unusual for natural history museums. Think of the life tableaux that were common just a few years ago and that can still be found in some institutions. We walk through a chamber of reconstructed dinosaur skeletons awed by the gigantic reptiles that once ruled the Earth, and enter a room filled with the strange people who inhabited America before it was discovered, so we are told, by Christopher Columbus. The Indians are mannequins, carefully molded to express the appropriate racial features. Dressed in traditional costumes and surrounded by glass cabinets containing their "artifacts," they are acting out some curator's conception of what life was like before European settlers arrived. Just as the dinosaurs are relics of a primitive and vanished time, so are the Indians. Indigenous people are displayed in their habitats, like other natural history specimens. That is perfectly understandable. After all, they were not civilized like we are. They were savages, from the Latin *silvaticus*, living like animals in the forest. Is it not true that many white Americans grew up being told not to "behave like wild Indians"? A group of school children walk into the room. They stare half in amazement and half in amusement at these figures strangely frozen in an eternal past. "So that is what 'wild' Indians were like!"

The present catalogue and exhibition reject this and similar methods of representing Native Americans and their culture. If we fully recognize indigenous people as the creators of artworks, then we will hardly be able to regard them as elements of the fauna and flora. But the decision to treat the material creations of Native Americans as works of art raises certain problems of its own.

Begin with a statement that seems to take away with one hand what it gives with the other: it is both misleading and necessary to refer to the material creations of Native Americans as works of art.

We can see that such a reference is misleading from simple linguistic consider-ations. There is no word synonymous with "art" in any Indian language, and this is not an accident. In the communities of North America prior to their alteration by European contact, art had not emerged as a specialized sphere of activity, separate from the rest of life. There were no museums, no galleries, no journals of art criticism, no auctions bringing astronomical bids. What we now call works of art were actually articles of use: baskets, textiles, pottery, instruments of warfare, ceremonial objects. It is therefore an anachronism to refer to them as works of art if, in so doing, we intend to distinguish them from more humble, utilitarian objects. The people who made and employed the items concerned made no such distinction themselves.

Still, we cannot help regarding the material creations of native cultures from the specialized artistic point of view now available to us. Artists are the only adults in our "advanced" Western society who, as a matter of course, use disciplined processes of fabrication to embody their deepest perceptions of the world in works that make those perceptions visible to others. And that is what native craftspeople do in the process of making ordinary functional objects. The same point can be made about song and dance. In native cultures, songs and dances are never artistic ends-in-themselves, since they always have some ritual or other purpose. And yet they communicate a depth of musical and motor awareness that establishes an affinity with the works of Western composers and choreographers.

This diorama of a Narragansett village was installed in 1917.
From the museum archives, circa 1958.

The art of indigenous North America is as subtle and varied as that of Europe. And yet there are certain significant differences in aesthetic perception between Western societies and traditional Indian communities. These are not distinctions in basic psychological functioning, however. In the first decades of the 20th century, it was common for both conservative detractors and avant-garde defenders of indigenous art to classify the thinking of native people together with that of children and the insane as a pre-rational alternative to the normal mental orientation of civilized adults. In *Primitive Art* (1927) and *The Primitive Mind of Man* (1938), the anthropologist Franz Boas tried to lay that pervasive Western myth to rest. In spite of the titles of his books, Boas was a critic of the concept of the "primitive." For him, all human communities have a full range of mental processes available among their members. It is just that particular cultures choose to accentuate certain of these processes rather than others. In other words, distinctions between Western and native aesthetic perceptions are matters of selective emphasis rather than fundamental differences in quality.

What, then, is the principal aesthetic difference between Native American art and the mainstream of the Western tradition as it flows from classical Greece and Rome through the Renaissance and into the art academies of the 19th and early 20th centuries? Art historians call this mainstream tradition "naturalism" and distinguish it, for example, from the very different experiments of modern art. In the most general terms, the indigenous art of North America is far less concerned with capturing the external appearance of objects than is European art in its dominant naturalistic version. It has little use for such illusionistic devices as perspective, modeling in light and shade, exact proportion and so on. Rather, the main task of Native American art is to convey what we might call the inner essence of its theme, and it approaches this task through the employment of conceptual, or symbolic, means.

Consider the wonderful Hopi kachina doll (page 55) collected by James Stevenson in the late 19th century on his famous expedition to the Southwest on behalf of the Smithsonian Institution, and now in the possession of the Museum of Natural History. The "doll" is not really a doll at all in any ordinary sense, but a ceremonial object presented to a child as a blessing. It is, of course, a manifestation of one of the kachinas, the spirits who come to dwell among the people in the form of masked dancers following the winter solstice. These impersonated spirits are vital to the communities they visit since, according to Hopi belief, they bring the return of rain to the arid Southwest. Rain, in turn, is necessary for the rebirth of corn and other cultivated plants among the people who depend upon them for survival.

Because the kachina doll in the museum's collection is quite early, it exhibits none of the compromises with Western naturalism that have produced the free-standing sculptures that contemporary collectors have come to prefer. Its body is flat, and its arms are painted on its rectangular torso instead of being carved independently. Its face is defined by a few simple lines painted on an elegant convex curve. The figure wears a headdress whose terraced pattern symbolizes rain clouds, as do its four painted semicircles. A jagged cut-out shape that splits each half of the headdress signifies lightning in the form of a stylized serpent. The artist has chosen not to represent the kachina naturalistically, the way in which a Renaissance sculptor might have shaped, say, a lifelike statue of a Christian angel. Instead, he has defined its image with a few markings that are abstractly conceptual, but that nevertheless evoke the regenerative power of rain.

If, in the presence of the kachina doll, we open not only our eyes but our hearts, then its underlying message becomes clear. The doll seems to insist that there is no point reproducing outer appearances because genuine reality is not located on the surface of things. The purpose of art is to create a visible symbol of the invisible realm of the spirit.

That message is also present in the visionary art of the Plains. Techniques for transforming ordinary consciousness into states of ecstatic awareness were common in the native communities of both North and South America. Often they involved the ingestion of hallucinogenic plants. But, apart from a limited employment of mescal beans and jimsom weed for the purpose of foretelling the future, hallucinogens were not in significant use among the Plains Indians until the rise of the peyote religion following the 19th-century destruction of native peoples and ways of life. Instead, in traditional Plains culture, visionary states were regularly induced as a part of the passage from puberty to adulthood by means of physical ordeal: fasting and thirsting, sensory deprivation and isolation in the wilderness.

Kachina Doll, Southwest, Pueblo, Hopi 1875-1925, Wood and pigments, 9 ¹/₂ in. long x 7 in. wide, Exchange; US National Museum.

After ritual purification in a sweatlodge, the teenage child was taken by a medicine man or woman deep into the forest, or to the top of a mountain or hill. There the child was left in a vision pit—a hole dug in the ground—with a blanket, perhaps a rattle, and nothing else. At this place, she (many girls as well as boys participated in the quest) remained alone for four days and nights, shivering, hungry and thirsty, often terrified at every random sound. If the quest were successful, the child would enter into an extraordinary state of awareness in which spirits appeared in the form of people or animals. They might take the child on a journey to the sky, brush her face with the wings of a bird, teach her a song, or deliver a message from a great grandparent. Whatever the nature of the experience might be, the vision, suitably interpreted by a medicine man or woman, provided the images and symbols from which she would draw power and guidance for the rest of her life. Moreover, the new adult would often record the vision by incorporating it into basketry, pottery, or clothing, or in the case of a man, painting it on a shield, shield cover, or the surface of a drum. In this way a tradition of visionary art took shape.

Since these images are so intensely personal, it is hard to identify with absolute certainty the objects in the museum's collection that exemplify them. But there is a drum whose surface depicts a buffalo dancer gazing into space (E 2208 7573). The dancer's line of sight encounters a large circular object suspended in mid-air and outlined in blue. This enigmatic image may very well symbolize a moment of ecstatic transcendence, a breakthrough to that side of the world which is normally hidden from view.

The museum possesses many items that do not record visionary experiences, but are nonetheless so charged with spiritual power that many Native Americans object to their exhibition or photographic reproduction. Among these are the pipes made for indigenous use. Though they do not appear in the catalogue or exhibition out of respect for their status as ceremonial objects, they are worth discussing anyway because of the light they shed on the nature of Native American material creations as works of art.

Most of the pipes are from the Plains. They come in two pieces: an exquisite, smoothly carved bowl shaped as an inverted "T," and a long wooden stem, sometimes decorated with beads, quills, feathers, and colorful pieces of cloth. The bowl represents the body of Mother Earth. Some believe that the red catlinite, or pipestone, quarried in order to make the bowl is the congealed blood of earlier generations of Plains peoples and of the bison they hunted. The stem represents the sky and has clearly male connotations. When the bowl and the stem are separated, they have no power. When joined together, they are spiritually charged and can be dangerous if not handled with the proper regard. But in this condition, they are able to carry prayers on clouds of tobacco smoke to the Powers that dwell in the four cardinal directions, and upward to what the Sioux call Wakan Tanka, the Great Mystery. The pipe connects its owner to the heart of the universe, to the generations that have come before, and to those that will follow.

Like the kachina doll and the visionary images of the Plains, we must regard the sacred pipe as a work of art. For it expresses a profound and subtle perception of the world in the form of a fabricated object. But we should also remember that the pipe differs in other ways from what the experts of our own society normally consider art. In its culture of origin, it was not meant to be a luxury commodity, to make the fortunes of dealers and the reputations of collectors, or to hang on the walls of museums. It was an inseparable part of a whole way of life, a way of life that found more important matters to be concerned with than the accumulation of money or the pursuit of careers. The poet and founder of the Surrealist movement, Andre Breton, once wrote that Native American objects possess a "convulsive beauty." We should take our lead from him. In order to appreciate the works in the museum's collection we must question our most basic presuppositions about the nature of art, and even about the nature of reality. If we let them, these incomparable works will shake us to the very core.

GARY ZABEL, PH.D., UNIVERSITY OF MASSACHUSETTS, BOSTON

CAPTION NOTES

The following explain the terms that accompany the objects.

OBJECT NAME

The common Anglo-European name for the object.

REGION AND TRIBE

Geographic location within North America and tribal name for Native Americans found within the specific geographic locale. Tribal and geographic origins that are uncertain are preceded by a question mark.

APPROXIMATE DATE MADE

Time period when the object was likely to have been fabricated, plus or minus twenty-five years.

MATERIALS OF CONSTRUCTION

The materials, such as leather, glass beads, wool fabric, wood, etc., used to make the objects.

SOURCE OF OBJECT

Name of collector, place of purchase or exchange.

MUSEUM CATALOGUE AND ACCESSION NUMBER

Multiple-digit number assigned to the object by the museum.

DESCRIPTION

Anthropological and aesthetic interpretive analysis of object.

Dimensions were taken from the longest, widest and highest points on the individual objects. Decorative fringe and tassels were included in the overall dimensions. Garments were measured from the center of the neck to the bottom hem and from sleeve-end to sleeve-end. In the case of sleeveless garments the width measurement was taken from arms-eye to arms-eye.

Catalogue analysis and captions were provided by Barbara A. Hail, Curator and Deputy Director, Haffenreffer Museum of Anthropology; Sarah Peabody Turnbaugh, Curator and Director, Museum of Primitive Art and Culture; Kristine L. Hastreiter, Associate Curator of Ethnology, Museum of Natural History.

FACING PAGE, FROM BACK TO FRONT

BOWL   SOUTHWEST, NEW MEXICO, (?)ACOMA 1850-1900
Ceramic, 3 ½ in. high x 7 in. diameter
Exchange; U.S. National Museum, E 2134 7483
Collected by James Stephenson (NO. 110669), Bureau
of American Ethnology, Smithsonian.

BOWL   SOUTHWEST, ARIZONA, HOPI 1860-1890
Ceramic, 3 in. high x 7 in. diameter
Exchange; U.S. National Museum, E 2138A
Collected by James Mooney (NO. 155305), Bureau of American
Ethnology, Smithsonian. In the Hopi region, many people tend to
regard the Historic Period, from 1650 to 1900, as one characterized
by decadent pottery, when the wares of this period are compared
to those of earlier periods. It was during this period, in the late 19th
century, that James Stevenson and James Mooney of the Bureau
of American Ethnology, Smithsonian, visited the Hopi region and
collected this example of Hopi pottery.

POLYCHROME BOWL   SOUTHWEST, NEW MEXICO, ZUNI
1860-1880
Ceramic, 3 ½ in. high x 9 ½ in. diameter
Exchange; U.S. National Museum, E 2135 7484
Collected by James Stevenson (NO. 11350) Bureau
of American Ethnology, Smithsonian.

POLYCHROME BOWL   SOUTHWEST, NEW MEXICO, ZUNI
c. 1890
Ceramic, 2 ¾ in. high x 6 ¾ in. diameter
Gift of Mrs. W. Fries, E 3605 11872

MOCCASINS   SUBARCTIC, CANADA, FORT PROVIDENCE
1915-1930
Leather and moose hair, 8 in. long x 3 ½ in. wide x 2 ½ in. high
Gift of Roland Hammond, E 2068 7394
These moccasins were given to Dr. Hammond by L. Romanet, who
was a general inspector for Hudson's Bay Company at Fort
McMurray in the Northwest Territories. The card that accompanies
these moccasins states that they were made by Mrs. Laferte of
Fort Providence. Mrs. Laferte is credited with inventing the craft
of moose hair tufting.

BASKET   NORTHWEST COAST, TSIMSHIAN STYLE
EARLY 20TH CENTURY
Cedar bark and bear grass, 5 ½ in. high x 5 ½ in. rim diameter
Gift of Walter G. Brown, E 2105 7453
The warm, mellow sheen of plaited cedar bark is accented with
black-dyed cedar and yellow-and-purple-dyed bear grass in an over-
lay technique called "beading," which–like a necklace–ornaments
and completes the overall appearance.

FACING PAGE, FROM LEFT TO RIGHT

DOLL   ARCTIC, LABRADOR, ESKIMO   1875-1925
Sealskin and wool, 7 ¼ in. long x 4 ½ in. wide
Gift of J.C. Kransnoff, E 1999 7148

DOLL   PLAINS OR WOODLAND   1850-1900
Leather, glass beads, and pigment, 5 in. long x 2 in. wide
Gift of Walter G. Brown, E 2196 7558

MINIATURE KAYAK   ARCTIC, ESKIMO   1850-1900
Wood, sinew and skin, 18 ½ in. long x 3 in. wide
Donor unknown, E 1102

DOLL   CENTRAL PLAINS   1885-1925
Leather and glass beads, 12 ¼ in. long x 5 ¾ in. circumference
Gift of H. A. Sweetland, E 3416 11644

FROM BACK TO FRONT

DIPPER   CENTRAL PLAINS, WYOMING, (?)ARAPAHO
1860-1917
Cow horn and glass beads, 12 ¾ in. long x 3 ⅜ in. wide
Gift of Walter G. Brown, E 4329
Natural materials of horn and wood were fashioned into containers
for gun powder or into scrapers or dippers. A horn spoon was made
by immersing the horn in warm water until it became pliable, then
slitting and opening it to the desired degree of flatness, and carving
the sides into a pleasing shape. Plains dippers were generally more
simple and functional, with only a slight attempt at decoration, typically in the form of incising and quill- or bead-wrapped handles.

DIPPER   BASIN, ROCKY MOUNTAINS, (?)UTE   1875-1925
Bighorn Sheep horn, 13 ½ in. long x 3 ¼ in. wide
Purchase; Providence Antique Company, E 2341 7953

DIPPER   NORTHWEST COAST, ALASKA, (?)HAIDA   1900-1931
Bone, 12 ¼ in. long x ½ in. wide
Gift of Mary C. P. Parker and Belle M. West, E 2407 8077

DIPPER   PLAINS   1875-1915
Cow horn and porcupine quills, 13 in. long x 3 ½ in. wide
Gift of Emily M. Thurber, E 375A 1832

DIPPER   NORTHEAST, EASTERN WOODLANDS   1850-1925
Wood, 7 ½ in. x 4 ¼ in. wide
Donor unknown, E 1964 4961
This carved wooden spoon has the initials "W. P." stamped or carved
into the handle. According to early records, Native Americans in
the New England area carried their own spoons. The initials on the
handle might have belonged to its owner.

DIPPER   NORTHWEST COAST, (?)ALASKA   1900-1931
Dall Sheep horn, 13 ¼ in. long x 3 ½ in. wide
Gift of Mary C. P. Parker and Belle M. West, E 2408 8078

DIPPER   NORTHWEST COAST   1875-1925
Mountain Goat horn, 8 in. long x 2 in. wide
Donor unknown, E 4226
This spoon was made by the Tlingit, Haida, or a neighboring
Northwest Coast tribe. It is inscribed with totem figures on the front
and back that may represent a halibut or killer whale motif.

DIPPER   BASIN, COLORADO, RUSSEL'S GULCH MINING
DISTRICT, (?)UTE   1825-1875
Bison horn, 11 in. long x 2 ½ in. wide
Gift of James Angus, E 852

LEFT, FROM TOP TO BOTTOM

BASKET PLAQUE   SOUTHWEST, HOPI 1920-1950
Yucca, 14 in. diameter
Gift of Alfred Whiting, E 3312 11532
A representational butterfly of indeterminate species surrounded by
an eight-petaled flower hovers at the center of this plaque from
Second Mesa. Wide, thick coils of yucca stitches in natural shades of
yellow and off-white are edged with red-orange and black-dyed yucca
to create the pattern.

BASKETRY TRAY   SOUTHWEST, HOPI 1940-1950
Rabbit brush, willow or sumac and yucca, 13 ½ in. diameter
Gift of Alfred Whiting, E 3310 11530
Plain plaited wicker basketry is made on westernmost Third Mesa,
the main pueblo of which is Oraibi. This tray could have been
used for corn meal in traditional rituals and ceremonies such as the
Basket Dance.

BASKETRY TRAY   SOUTHWEST, HOPI EARLY 20TH CENTURY
Yucca, 13 ½ in. diameter
Donor unknown, E 4326
Yucca in natural shades and dyed black, green, and red has been used
to create this older, traditional design. Basket makers on Second
Mesa have created these bundle coiled trays for generations; they are
used for corn meal in ancient rituals and ceremonies such as the
Basket Dance.

FACING PAGE

JACKET   SUBARCTIC, CANADA, FORT PEEL 1900-1930
Moose hide, silk embroidery and wool trim
Gift of Roland Hammond, E 2075 7401
This coat of smoked moose hide, hand-pinked wool trim, and hand-
sewn seams, is embroidered with silk thread in a buttonhole stitch.
It is unlined and has a yoke with straight-cut fringe. It resembles the
"Norway House style" jackets that were popular in the Lake
Winnipeg area of the Northwest Territories at the turn of the century.

BUCKSKIN PANTS   PLAINS OR PLATEAU 1875-1925
Buckskin and glass beads, 44 in. long x 41 in. wide
Gift of Walter G. Brown, E 2189 7551
These hand-sewn yellow buckskin pants are embellished with floral
beadwork and fringe.

FACING PAGE, CLOCKWISE FROM TOP LEFT

BAG   GREAT LAKES, NEW YORK, IROQUOIS 1875-1900
Cotton velveteen and glass beads, 7 ¼ in. long x 6 in. wide
Purchase; Providence Antique Company, E 2338 7950

SMOKING CAP   GREAT LAKES, NEW YORK, IROQUOIS
1850-1925
Cotton velveteen and glass beads, 11 ½ in. long x 5 ½ in. wide x
3 ½ in. high
Gift of Mrs. Abram Manchester, E 1909 2704
During the fur trade era, Iroquois Indians came in contact with
Scotsmen who wore uniquely shaped bonnets identified with
the Glengarry region of Scotland. The Iroquois appreciated the
form, and adapted it to their own taste, adding characteristic
floral appliqué beadwork.

NEEDLE CASE   GREAT LAKES, NEW YORK, IROQUOIS
1875-1925
Cotton velveteen and glass beads, 7 in. long x 4 in. wide
Donor unknown, E 4221
This needle case held sewing tools at one time. The padded center
section is for straightpins; the muslin was probably for needles;
and the pockets held thread and other sewing paraphernalia.

CHILD'S MOCCASINS   GREAT LAKES, NEW YORK, IROQUOIS
1875-1925
Leather, cotton velveteen and glass beads, 5 ½ in. long x
3 ½ in. wide x 2 ¾ in. high
Donor unknown, E 4218
Moccasins were worn by the Iroquois, but also were sold as
souvenirs to tourists who came to such attractions as Niagara Falls
and Saratoga Springs. Iroquois appliqué beadwork can be found
on a variety of items such as clothing, bags, hats and decorative
ornaments called "whimseys." Typically, color schemes and designs
were similar; however, individual stylistic variations flourished.

PICTOGRAPH HIDE   PLAINS, WYOMING, SHOSHONE
ARTIST: CHADZI CODY, 1850-1900
Bovid hide and pigment, 77 in. long x 75 in. wide
Gift of Walter G. Brown, E 2354 7966
Some skin paintings tell a story of the exploits of the artist and
serve as a kind of diary. Others describe historic tribal events or recall
particular ceremonies. Without the artist's explanation it is
difficult to tell exactly what is depicted in a painting. This painted
hide illustrates a buffalo hunt and the Sun Dance. The pictograph conventions used do not show influence of Western art styles
(e.g., riders have only one leg and the torsos face outward).

BOOTS   ARCTIC, LABRADOR, ESKIMO CIRCA 1927
Deerskin soles and sealskin uppers, 12 in. long x 5 in. wide x
18 ½ in. high
Gift of J. C. Kransnoff, E 2014 7162
These boots, called muk-luks by the Eskimos, were collected
in 1927 by J. C. Kransnoff, who was working as a dentist at the
International Grenfell Mission, Labrador.

BANDOLIER BAG   GREAT LAKES, WISCONSIN, WINNEBAGO
OR MENOMINEE 1850-1925
Wool, silk and glass beads, 41 in. long x 11 in. wide
Purchase; Providence Antique Company, E 1905 2647
Great Lakes Indians adapted the bandolier bag from ammunition
pouches that European soldiers carried during the 18th century.
Bandolier bags were worn over the shoulder and across the chest,
so that the decorated pouch area hung down at one's side. The
bags were made to be decorative rather than functional; many of
the later examples do not have a usable pouch. They were treasured
items and were often given as gifts. They were sometimes referred
to as "friendship bags."

FACING PAGE, FROM LEFT TO RIGHT

PIPE BAG   CENTRAL PLAINS 1875-1925

Leather, glass beads and porcupine quills, 38 in. long x 7 ½ in. wide

Donor unknown, E 4325

A variety of skin bags were used by both men and women on the Plains for multiple purposes. Men carried decorative tubular pipe bags large enough to hold both tobacco and a pipe bowl. The ideas for decorating a man's bag were conceived by its owner, although the quill and bead stitchery were executed by women.

PIPE BAG   CENTRAL/NORTHERN PLAINS 1875-1925

Leather, glass beads and porcupine quills, 35 in. long x 6 ½ in. wide

Gift of Walter G. Brown, E 2195 7557

Glass beads with a metallic finish and translucent beads were popular in the last quarter of the 19th century and the first quarter of the 20th century. The beaded section of this bag was made separately from the top of the bag. The original top was probably worn out and replaced, hence the colors and designs of the three sections of the bag do not flow together aesthetically. The top of the fringed section has been cut with a pinking shears, a favorite sewing tool of Plains tribes. The beaded "feathered circle" motif, found on the backside of this bag, was often used by Assiniboine/Teton Sioux, especially in painted robe designs.

PIPE BAG   CENTRAL PLAINS, TETON SIOUX TYPE
1875-1925

Leather, glass beads and porcupine quills, 32 ½ in. long x 7 in. wide

Gift of Ellen M. Anthony, E 1901 2645

CALLING CARD TRAY   NORTHEAST, HURON 1800-1875

Birch bark and moose hair, 7 ¾ in. diameter

Gift of Lydia S. Talbot, E 1797 2324

This finely worked tray is made of birch bark and moose hair. It is modeled after Victorian calling card trays used for leaving word of a visit. Moose hair embroidery items like this were made expressly for sale by Huron girls of Lorette Mission, Quebec, who developed the craft with Ursuline nuns in the 18th century.

CLOCKWISE, FROM LEFT REAR BASKET

RATTLE-TOP BASKET   NORTHWEST COAST, TLINGIT STYLE
EARLY 20TH CENTURY
Spruce root and bear grass, 6 ¾ in. high x 3 in. diameter
Gift of Walter G. Brown, E 2097 7445
The patterns on this basket suggest looking into water. Green
design elements depict the shadow of a little tree reflected in
rippling water, while the orange lozenge pattern probably represents
the splash made when a raindrop hits a smooth surface. Small
pebbles or lead shot were placed in the lid rattle, perhaps to mimic
the sound of gently falling rain.

BASKET   NORTHWEST COAST, TLINGIT 1875-1917
Spruce root and bear grass, 5 ¼ in. high x 6 ½ in. diameter
Gift of Walter G. Brown, E 2093 7441
The orca or killer whale element was initially adapted from Chilkat
blanket designs. The Tlinglit began to use this popular animal on
baskets for sale to tourists in the second or third decades of the
20th century. This example of the black and white orca is especially
complex and interesting.

RATTLE-TOP BASKET   NORTHWEST COAST, TLINGIT STYLE
EARLY 20TH CENTURY
Spruce root and maidenhair fern, 3 in. high x 4 ½ in. diameter
Gift of Walter G. Brown, E 2096 7444
This small covered basket has a chamber in the lid in which tiny
stones or shot have been enclosed to create a rattle. It was
probably made for sale to tourists as a trinket basket. The dark
false embroidered design is the butterfly, an outline of the
insect's open wings. Triangular elements represent half the head
of a salmonberry, a fruit like a salmon-colored raspberry.

BASKET   NORTHWEST COAST, TLINGIT STYLE
EARLY 20TH CENTURY
Spruce root and bear grass, 6 in. long x ¾ in. wide x 6 ½ in. high
Gift of Walter G. Brown, E 2098 7446
Mellow white and faded gold tones of bear grass on spruce root
give this flat case a rich, golden glow. The "blanket border" fret
design and crossed warp twining create an especially dressy finish.
This basket may have served as a spoon bag, which, when hung
on a wall, would hold spoons made from mountain goat horns.

BASKET   NORTHWEST COAST
LATE 19TH-EARLY 20TH CENTURY
Spruce root and bear grass, 2 ¾ in. high x 4 ¼ in. diameter
Donor unknown, E 4225
The scene depicts hunting from a native boat called an umiak.
An orca has been snagged on a line, while two green fish placidly
float by. Whaling was a prestigious activity in the Northwest
Coast, and whalers were always of the noble class.

BASKET   NORTHWEST COAST, TLINGIT STYLE
EARLY 20TH CENTURY
Spruce root, bear grass and maidenhair fern, 5 ½ in. high x
6 in. diameter
Gift of Walter G. Brown, E 2095 7443
Twined of spruce root and false embroidered with two fretwork
bands of black maidenhair fern in a Hudson's Bay Company
"blanket border" pattern, this basket also sports a row of red-dyed
bear grass "crosses" or "kuh-naste." The cross motif was adopted
relatively recently, in the early 20th century, and is credited
to the Russian Orthodox Church; Russian fur traders and hunters
regularly traveled the Northwest Coast of North America through-
out the 19th century.

STORAGE BOX   NORTHWEST COAST, TLINGIT 1900-1950
Cedar wood, 15 in. wide x 16 in. deep x 14 ¾ in. high
Exchange; Dartmouth College, E 3683 12003
On the Northwest Coast, boxes were used for many different purposes and were made in many sizes. They served both utilitarian
and ceremonial functions. Typically, boxes were made out of cedar,
and the sides were carved from one plank of wood, which was
kerfed, steamed and bent at the corners. The first and fourth sides
were pegged or sewn together. The bottom of a box was a separate
piece of cedar that was attached with pegs.

MINIATURE TOTEM POLE   NORTHWEST COAST, (?)ALASKA
1875-1925
Cedar wood and pigment, 25 in. high x 15 in. circumference
Donor unknown, E 2086 7434

RATTLE   NORTHWEST COAST, BRITISH COLUMBIA,
HAIDA STYLE 1875-1925
Wood, 15 in. long x 12 ½ in. circumference
Donor unknown, E 2087 7435
Tiny pebbles or lead shot have been enclosed between two pieces
of wood that were carved and sewn together to create this chief's
rattle, or "sasawkh." The formline carving is painted black for pri-
mary forms, red for secondary, and blue for tertiary, and the overall
carving depicts a raven with a human reclining on its back, facing
a frog. The human's tongue is joined to the frog, in a representation
of transference of power from one to another. On the rounded
underside of the rattle, carved on the raven's breast, is the image of
a sparrow hawk. Raven rattles were primarily used by chiefs or
headmen during social ceremonies.

CREST HAT   NORTHWEST COAST, QUEEN CHARLOTTE
ISLANDS, HAIDA STYLE LATE 19TH CENTURY
Sitka spruce root and pigments, 7 ½ in. high x 14 in. diameter
Exchange; Museum of the American Indian, E 1179 2216
Black, red, and blue pigments have been used to paint elaborate
totemic designs, typical of the Northwest Coast formline art style,
on the surface of this crest hat. Made for and worn by the wealthy
class, crest hats were painted with stylized animal representations
that symbolized the owner's clan affiliation. The animal depicted
on this hat is most likely a wolf, with prominent nostrils, long
muzzle, and forepaws.

POLYCHROME SEED JAR   SOUTHWEST, NEW MEXICO,
ZIA OR ACOMA 1875-1925
Ceramic, 7 in. high x 9½ in. diameter
Donor unknown, E 4331

CALLING CARD CASE   NORTHEAST, EASTERN WOODLANDS,
(?) MALISEET   1850-1900
Wool felt, silk ribbon and glass beads, 6 ½ in. long x 5 ¼ in. wide
Donor unknown, E 4220
This double-sided, wallet-style case was made for sale to tourists
and was probably used to carry calling cards.

FACING PAGE, CLOCKWISE FROM LEFT TOP

POUCH   ARCTIC, GREENLAND, ESKIMO 1900-1945
Sealskin, 17 in. long (includes strap) x 10 in. wide
Gift of Raymond Vaughn, E 3070A

MOCCASINS   ARCTIC, GREENLAND, ESKIMO 1875-1950
Sealskin, 10 ¾ in. long x 3 ½ in. wide x 3 ⅜ in. high
Gift of Raymond Vaughn, E 3070E 11122
These moccasins were worn by a woman as indoor footwear. They
are made of sealskin turned inside out. Note the decorative appliqué.

POUCH   ARCTIC, GREENLAND, ESKIMO 1900-1925
Sealskin and mink appliqué, 13 in. long (includes handle) x
9 ½ in. wide
Gift of Raymond Vaughn, E 3070B

MOCCASINS   ARCTIC, GREENLAND, ESKIMO 1875-1950
Sealskin, 10 in. long x 3 in. wide x 3 in. high
Gift of Raymond Vaughn, E 3070D 71122

RUG SOUTHWEST, NAVAJO 1900-1950

Wool and cotton, 86 in. long x 62 in. wide

Gift of Everet W. Freeman, E 4328

The extremely unusual design and color combination of this rug
suggest that it may have been a commissioned piece. The warp is
two-ply, "s" twist, commercial cotton thread. The weft is single-ply
handspun wool colored with aniline dyes.

MOCCASINS   PLAINS, CHEYENNE 1875-1940
Leather and glass beads, 11 in. long x 4 in. wide x 4 in. high
Gift of Mrs. R. H. Whitmarsh, E 3094 11299
Early 19th century Northern Plains moccasins had soft soles made
of one piece of tanned skin folded around the foot. Hard soles
of rawhide were added to one-piece soft sole moccasins during the
mid-19th century. The hard sole was originally added as a second
sole sewn to the outside of a one-piece moccasin. Later the moccasin
was made in two pieces. Each of the four pairs of moccasins pictured
here is made of a hard rawhide sole sewn to a soft buckskin upper.

MOCCASINS   NORTH CENTRAL PLAINS, CROW 1890-1917
Leather and glass beads, 10 ½ in. long x 3 ½ in. wide x 4 ½ in. high
Gift of Walter G. Brown, E 2175 7533

MOCCASINS   CENTRAL PLAINS, SOUTH DAKOTA,
BLACK HILLS 1875-1925
Leather and glass beads, 10 in. long x 3 ¾ in. x 3 ½ in. high
Donor unknown, E 2179 7541
These moccasins were collected in the Black Hills of South Dakota
and are probably Cheyenne, Arapaho, or Teton Sioux in origin.

MOCCASINS   CENTRAL PLAINS, TETON SIOUX TYPE
1875-1925
Leather, glass beads, cotton gingham and horse hair tinklers,
10 in. long x 3 ¾ in. wide x 4 in. high
Gift of Charles F. Stearns, E 2019 7173
The four pairs of beaded moccasins pictured here are representative
of the form and traditional design ubiquitous among the Plains
tribes. Variations on these and other beaded designs are unique to
the artisan.

BASKET   NORTHWEST COAST, CASCADES, SALISHAN
EARLY 20TH CENTURY
Cedar bark, spruce root and bear grass, 7 in. high x 7 in. wide x
9 in. (oval) diameter
Donor unknown, E 2110 7458
This basket form was popular among Salishan peoples such as the
Skokomish, Quinault, and nearby groups, inhabiting the general
region along and around the Pacific Coast and Columbia River from
Washington State to British Columbia. The scalloped rim accenting
the row of seven dogs below provides a charming and fun touch.

FACING PAGE, CLOCKWISE FROM REAR

POLYCHROME JAR (OLLA)   SOUTHWEST, NEW MEXICO,
ACOMA OR (?) ZIA   1875-1925
Ceramic, 10 in. high x 13 in. diameter
Exchange; U.S. National Museum, E 2138 7487
Collected by James Stevenson (NO.110163), Bureau of American
Ethnology, Smithsonian. The late 19th century was a period when
relatively few Pueblo ceramics were produced. The decline of this
artistic tradition was the result of encroachment by non-Indians
onto Pueblo lands. During the early 20th century several revivals of
Pueblo ceramic art occurred. The sale of pottery outside the pueblos
provided a source of income, and in a relatively short time, Pueblo
pottery changed from a "curio" sales item to an *objet d'art*. Today, a
number of the pueblos produce fine ceramics.

POLYCHROME JAR   SOUTHWEST, NEW MEXICO, ACOMA
1900-1950
Ceramic, 7 ¾ in. high x 4 ¾ in. diameter
Gift of J. Carrington, E 3377 11604

STEPPED BOWL   SOUTHWEST, NEW MEXICO, ZUNI
1850-1900
Ceramic, 4 ½ in. high x 6 ¾ in. diameter
Exchange; U.S. National Museum, E 2136 7485
Collected by James Stevenson (NO.40388), Bureau of American
Ethnology, Smithsonian

MINIATURE POLYCHROME JAR   SOUTHWEST, NEW MEXICO,
ZIA 1890-1910
Ceramic, 2 ½ in. high x 2 ⅛ in. diameter
Donor unknown, E 4327

SADDLE BLANKET   SOUTHWEST, TEEC NOS POS AREA,
NAVAJO 1875-1915
Wool and cotton, 28 in. long x 32 in. wide
Gift of Walter G. Brown, E 2214 7646
Navajo textiles can be traced to their origin of manufacture by
aesthetic attributes. This is possible because certain trading post
centers produced rugs of distinctive style, pattern and color.
Teec Nos Pos textiles, such as this one, feature an "outline design,"
in which every design element (diamonds, squares, slashes, etc.)
is outlined by a second color.

MINATURE CARVINGS   ARCTIC, ESKIMO 1875-1918
Ivory, *Polar Bear*: 6 ¼ in. long x 1 ¼ in. wide x 2 in. high;
Ducks: 1 in. long x ¾ in. wide x ⅞ in. high; ¾ in. long x
¾ in. wide x ¾ in. high
Gift of (?) Daniel B. Fearing, E 150A,B,C
Hand-carved miniature animals in the shapes of ducks
and polar bear.

MINIATURE CARVINGS   ARCTIC, ALASKA, ESKIMO 1875-1925
Ivory, *Figure*: 1 ⅝ in. long x ¾ in. wide; *Sled*: 1 ⅞ in. long x
½ in. wide
Gift of J. Arthur Edward, E 2441 8493
Miniature objects such as this dog sled and driver were often
made as "curios" for sale to tourists.

TOOLS   ARCTIC, ALASKA, NORTON SOUND, ESKIMO
1875-1918
Ivory, 5 ⅜ in. long x ½ in. wide; 4 ¼ in. long x ½ in. wide
Gift of Daniel B. Fearing, E 1081A,B

TOOLS   ARCTIC, ALASKA, NORTON SOUND, ESKIMO
1875-1918
Ivory, 3 ½ in. long x ⅜ in. wide
Gift of Daniel B. Fearing, E 1082A,B
These tools were used to crease walrus hide to make boots,
called muk-luks.

MINIATURE POCKET KNIFE   ARCTIC, ALASKA, NORTON
SOUND, ESKIMO 1875-1918
Ivory, 2 ⅜ in. long x ⅜ in. wide
Gift of Daniel B. Fearing, E 1084A 189

MINIATURE CARVINGS   ARCTIC, ALASKA, NORTON SOUND,
ESKIMO 1875-1918
Ivory, 3 ⅝ in. long x ½ in. wide; 2 ⅛ in. long x ⅜ in. wide
Gift of Daniel B. Fearing, E 1084B,C 189
Hand-carved in the shape of fish.

THIMBLE   ARCTIC, ESKIMO 1875-1925
Ivory, ¾ in. high x ¾ in. diameter
Donor unknown, E 2046A

FISH HOOK   ARCTIC, ALASKA, NORTON SOUND, ESKIMO
1850-1900
Ivory and iron, 1 ⅞ in. long x ⅜ in. wide
Gift of Daniel B. Fearing, E 1068 189
Bering Sea Eskimo implements were designed to be pleasing to
the animal and natural spirits with which the implements would
be associated in use. Harpoon points and fish hooks were often
ornamented with delicate designs in which the circle-dot motif
was prominent.

FISH HOOK   ARCTIC, ALASKA, NORTON SOUND, ESKIMO
1850-1900
Walrus ivory and steel, 3 in. long x ⅛ in. wide
Gift of Daniel B. Fearing, E 1064

FISH HOOK   ARCTIC, ALASKA, NORTON SOUND, ESKIMO
1850-1900
Walrus ivory, glass bead, iron, and auklet bill fragment, 3 ⅝ in.
long x ½ in. wide; 2 ⅛ in. long x ⅜ in. wide
Gift of Daniel B. Fearing, E 1062 189
Eskimo fishermen crafted different types of lures and sinkers for
catching tomcod, grayling and other fish. Spiked composite hooks,
such as this hook, were for tomcod. Glass beads and orange-colored
auklet bill fragments served as bait.

SEWING KIT   ARCTIC, VICTORIA ISLAND, ESKIMO
1850-1900
Ivory, 4 in. long x 2 ½ in. wide
Gift of A.H. Anderson Collection, E 2046 7200

CARIBOU TEETH   ARCTIC, CANADA, CORONATION GULF,
ESKIMO 1850-1900
Caribou, each tooth approximately 1 ¼ to 1 ½ in. long x ¼ in. wide
Gift of A.H. Anderson, E 2059 7213
Animal teeth served a variety of functions in Native American
culture. Caribou teeth were used by the Eskimos to make fishing
lures and decorate clothing.

VEST   CENTRAL PLAINS   1875-1910
Cloth, leather and glass beads, 15 ½ in. long x 16 in. wide
Gift of Walter G. Brown, E 2176 7538
This child's vest features a design of lines and hooks, a pattern
prevalent after 1870. The beaded design incorporates glass beads
as well as metallic facet beads, which were used from 1885-95.

BASKET   SOUTHWEST, PIMA CIRCA 1900
Willow, martynia and cattail, 3 in. high x 13 in. diameter
Donor unknown, E 3758 12087
This complex, maze-like meander or fret design and the false-braid
rim finish are typical of late 19th-early 20th-century Pima work.
During manufacture, the basket maker pounded the coils on this
basket to flatten them and give them a smooth, finished appearance.

BASKET   SOUTHWEST, PIMA 1890-1915
Willow, martynia and cattail, 3 in. high x 9 in. diameter
Donor unknown, E 3757 12080
A radiating whorl or fret design in black martynia against natural-
colored willow stitches over a bundle foundation of cattail stems
team up with the narrow base and flaring walls to give this tray an
appearance of motion, fluidity, and lightness.

BASKET   SOUTHWEST, WESTERN APACHE 1890-1910
Willow, cottonwood and martynia, 4 in. high x 9 in. diameter
Donor unknown, E 3756 12085
A double five-pointed star or flower design element sets off five
groups of three stylized dogs or "scotties." Baskets with representa-
tional life forms were popular among turn-of-the-century tourists.

BASKET   SOUTHWEST, PAPAGO OR PIMA
EARLY 20TH CENTURY
Willow and martynia, 3 in. high x 7 in. diameter
Donor unknown, E 3760 12089
This small basket, decorated with five stylized male figures, was a
sale item for tourists. Human figures and life forms were favorite
basketry design elements at the turn of the century and are equally
popular today.

JACKET   ARCTIC, GREENLAND, ESKIMO 1875-1945
Sealskin and cotton, 30 in. long x 58 in. wide
Gift of Raymond Vaughn, E 3070 10825
The cut of this jacket is an imitation of European-style jackets.
The open front, buttons, and muslin lining all indicate that the
item may have been made for a tourist or visitor. In general,
Eskimos used sealskin for summer and caribou for winter clothing.

HORSE ORNAMENT   PLAINS, CROW 1885-1910
Wool, glass beads, metal sequins and brass bells, 51 ¾ in. long x
17 in. wide
Gift of Henry D. Sharpe, E 2348 175
Skillfully worked of red wool obtained from traders, along with
glass beads, metal sequins and brass bells, this horse collar typically
adorned Crow Indian horses. It was worn around the horse's neck
so that the large portion hung across the chest.

SHIRT   PLAINS 1875-1917

Leather, porcupine quills and horse hair, 27 ½ in. long x 56 in. wide
Gift of Walter G. Brown, E 2190 7552

Deer-leg shirts, also called war shirts, were worn until the mid-19th
century by distinguished leaders as a kind of honorary emblem.
Made from two skins of deer, elk, antelope, bighorn sheep, or small
buffalo, these shirts were highly decorated with paintings of
their owners' war exploits, small bunches of human or horse hair
representative of scalp trophies taken, and strips of woven and plaited porcupine quills sewn on at the shoulders and upper sleeves.
After the second half of the 19th century, war shirts continued to be
made but they became common apparel for men. The common
Central Plains style is a poncho with open sides, with a neck flap in
a triangular shape and sleeves sewn from wrist to elbow. Among
the Teton Sioux, shirts are typically painted two colors. The top half
is blue for sky, the bottom half red or yellow for earth. They often
have decorative bands of quill embroidery in geometric designs.

FACING PAGE, FROM BACK TO FRONT

LIDDED BASKET   ARCTIC, ALEUT (PROBABLY ATTU)
LATE 19TH CENTURY
Wild rye grass, 4 in. high x 5 ½ in. diameter
Gift of Walter G. Brown, E 2089 7437
Decorative bands of diverted warp twining and embroidered
geometric elements embellish this finely woven trinket basket.
Wild rye grass was gathered close at hand, near the sea. It was then
prepared and split into thin elements for twining the linen-like
baskets. The Aleut basket makers worked in their homes near the
Arctic Circle, where the sun does not shine for about half of
each year.

LIDDED BASKET   LOWER NORTHWEST COAST, NOOTKA
(PROBABLY NITINAT BAND) LATE 19TH-EARLY 20TH CENTURY
Cedar bark, bear grass and dyes, 2 ½ in. high x 4 in. diameter
Gift of Walter G. Brown, E 2112 7460

LIDDED BASKET   LOWER NORTHWEST COAST,
NOOTKA (PROBABLY NITINAT BAND) LATE 19TH-EARLY
20TH CENTURY
Cedar bark, bear grass and dyes, 3 in. high (with knob) x
2 ½ in. diameter
Donor unknown, E 3754 12083
Orange and purple geometric elements balance a carefully and
expertly twined purple knob atop the lid. High stitch counts
of 20 and 24 stitches per inch and 26 courses or rows per inch
indicate that these fine baskets were probably made by members
of the Wakashan-speaking Nitinat band of the Nootka, on
Vancouver Island.

KACHINA DOLL   SOUTHWEST, PUEBLO, HOPI 1875-1925
Wood and pigments, 9 ½ in. long x 7 in. wide
Exchange; U.S. National Museum, E 2117 7466

MODEL TIPI   NORTH CENTRAL PLAINS, NORTH DAKOTA,
STANDING ROCK RESERVATION 1875-1885
Wood, leather and glass beads, 50 in. high x 44 in. diameter
Gift of Charles Abbot, E 3357 11578
Toys such as model tipis, miniature bows and arrows, dolls and
model cradles were put to use in imitative learning. Every boy had
to know how to hunt; every girl had to know how to cut out skin
clothing, make cradles, and sew together the skins for a tipi. Plains
tipis are of either three-pole or four-pole construction. This is the
number of poles that are tied together initially and used to raise the
tipi into position. The remaining poles are placed in a circle resting
on the outside of the original group. The ears, or flaps, which prevent
wind and rain from entering the smoke hole, are held in place by
two longer poles. The beaded hoops on this tipi typically symbolized
tribal unity, four directions or life force, and were commonly placed
on the four sides of Cheyenne and Arapaho tipis as protective devices.

BIBLIOGRAPHY

Collier, D. and Tschopik, H. " The Role of Museums in American Anthropology," *American Anthropology*, 56 (5, Part 1) pp. 768-779, 1954.

Denton, P. Lynn. *The Second Century: Anthropology in Natural History Museums,* "In Natural History Museums: Directions for Growth," pp. 213-237. Paisley S. Cato, Clyde Jones (Editors). Texas Tech University, 1991.

Dittert, Alfred E., Jr. and Fred Plog. *Generations in Clay Pueblo Pottery of the American Southwest*, Northland Publishing: Flagstaff, Arizona, 1980.

Dockstader, Frederik, J. *Indian Art in North America*, New York Graphic Society, Greenwich, Connecticut, 1961.

Gordon, Beverly and Melanie Herzog. *American Indian Art: The Collecting Experience*, University of Wisconsin Press, Madison, Wisconsin, 1988.

Hail, Barbara and Kate Duncan. *Out of the North*, Haffenreffer Museum of Anthropology, Bristol, Rhode Island, 1989.

Hail, Barbara. *Hau, Kóla!* Haffenreffer Museum of Anthropology, Bristol, Rhode Island, 1989.

Hill, Tom and Richard W. Hill Sr. (Editors). *Creation's Journey: Native American Identity and Belief*, Smithsonian Institution Press, Washington, D.C., 1994.

Karp, Ivan. "Culture and Representation," *Exhibiting Cultures the Poetics and Politics of Museum Display*, Smithsonian Institution Press, Washington, D.C., 1991.

Maxwell, Gilbert S. *Navajo Rugs—Past, Present & Future*, Desert-Southwest, Inc., Palm Desert, California, 1963.

Marshall, David. *Jewel of Providence*, Providence Parks Department, Providence, Rhode Island, 1987.

Minutes of the Board of Park Commissioners, January 7, 1994.

Osgood, C. *Anthropology in Museums of Canada and the United States*, Milwaukee Public Museum, Milwaukee, Wisconsin, 1979.

Sheets-Pyenson, Susan. *Cathedrals of Science: The Development of Colonial Natural History Museums in the Late 19th Century*, McGill-Queens University Press, Montreal, Quebec, 1988.

"The People's Pleasure Ground: Roger Williams Park Providence," The American Book Exchange, 1897-98.

Walters, Anna Lee. *The Spirit of Native America*, Chronical Books, San Francisco, 1989.

Wardwell, Allen. *Objects of Bright Pride*, Center for Inter-American Relations, New York, 1978.

INDEX

The Museum of Natural History is connected to its natural landscape, 1995.

PROJECT TEAM

Tracey K. Brussat
Museum Director

Marilyn Massaro
Curator of Collections

Judith K. Sweeney
Curator of Education

Kristine L. Hastreiter
Associate Curator of Ethnology
Exhibition Designer

Joanne Wilcox
Administrative Assistant

Design
Nicole Juen Studio
Providence, Rhode Island

Photography
Ira Garber Photography
Providence, Rhode Island

Production Manager
Susan McNally
Boston, Massachusetts

Copyediting
David Brussat
Providence, Rhode Island

Printing
Meridian Printing
East Greenwich, Rhode Island